PRE-WAR STEAM

Richard Denny

AMBERLEY

First published 2018

Amberley Publishing
The Hill, Stroud
Gloucestershire, GL5 4EP

www.amberley-books.com

ISBN 978 1 4456 8399 7 (print)
ISBN 978 1 4456 8400 0 (ebook)

British Library Cataloguing in Publication Data.
A catalogue record for this book is available from
the British Library.

Origination by Amberley Publishing.
Printed in the UK.

Introduction

Railways have been of interest to me for a continuous period of almost sixty years. As a child I was more into planes and space travel, however, and despite attending my junior school, which was opposite Northampton loco shed, and which from certain classrooms loco movements on and off shed could clearly be seen, they failed to evoke much interest, though I was aware that many of the boys and one or two girls had these small books, which I later found to be famous Ian Allan spotting books. At about ten years old I did eventually join the spotting fraternity and have retained that railway interest to the present day – although the scene is much less interesting than it once was.

Recent years have led to the collection of many slides and photographs, as well as an increasing interest in pre-war railways, which previously would have been completely outside my realm of curiosity. Apart from the problem of selecting a variety of historic photographs of good enough quality, I have derived a lot of pleasure in researching information about the locomotives, some of which have come from trusted publications and none from the internet – which can contain dodgy 'facts'.

Although the book does contain a number of images of main line express engines, I have deliberately tried to include more of the everyday type of unsung classes – within the scope of the book, of course – and there are well over 100 different types contained within. As the largest of the pre-nationalisation companies, the LMSR is naturally best represented, with the GWR, LNER and Southern represented proportionally based on their locomotive fleet size.

I sincerely hope this first offering of mine will prove enjoyable and that it will be possible to do another in the future.

Richard Denny
Northampton
July 2018

Abbreviations Used

BR – British Railways
CME – Chief Mechanical Engineer
CR – Caledonian Railway
GER – Great Eastern Railway
GNR – Great Northern Railway
GNOSR – Great North of Scotland Railway
GSWR – Glasgow & South Western Railway
GWR – Great Western Railway
HR – Highland Railway
LBSCR – London Brighton & South Coast Railway
LCDR – London Chatham & Dover Railway
LMSR – London Midland & Scottish Railway
LNWR – London & North Western Railway
L&Y – Lancashire & Yorkshire Railway
LNER – London & North Eastern Railway
LSWR – London & South Western Railway
LTSR – London Tilbury & Southend Railway
MR – Midland Railway
M&GNR – Midland & Great Northern Railway
M&SWR – Midland & South Western Railway
NBR – North British Railway
NER – North Eastern Railway
NLR – North London Railway
RJB – Ron. J. Buckley
S&DJR – Somerset & Dorset Joint Railway
SECR – South Eastern & Chatham Railway
SER – South Eastern Railway
SR – Southern Railway

No. 9205, one of Bowen Cooke's G1 Class 0-8-0s (a development of F. Whale's G Type), stands at Rugby shed. The G1 was rated at 6F and rendered good service to the LNWR and later the LMS. The last examples were not withdrawn until 1964. 236 locos of this class were built.

Johnson MR 0-6-0T No. 1857 at Brightside in July 1938. 280 of these diminutive engines were constructed between 1874 and 1900 and many enjoyed long lives, the last five not being withdrawn until 1966, including No. 41708, which was then eighty-six years old. No. 41857 was withdrawn in 1959 after a useful sixty-four years of service.

4-6-0 No. 4092 *Dunraven Castle* heads a Paddington-bound express at Twyford. The Castle Class was C. B. Collett's development of Churchward's Star 4-6-0 and stood second only to the King Class in the GWR express power classification. No. 4092 was built in 1925 and was withdrawn in late 1964, being quickly scrapped at Swindon works.

A1 (later A3) Class 4-6-2 No. 2500 *Windsor Lad*, a member of the well-known class that includes the famous *Flying Scotsman*. No. 2500 was named after the Maharaja of Rajpipla's racehorse, winner of the 1934 Derby and St Leger. Renumbered to 35 then 60035, *Windsor Lad* was allocated to Haymarket shed for much of its life, being withdrawn in September 1961.

GWR 4-6-0 No. 4001 *Dog Star*. The Star Class was designed by George Jackson Churchward and the seventy-three locomotives that made up the class were built between 1906 and 1923. Known as very free running engines, No. 4001 itself was built in February 1907 and was withdrawn in January 1934, having run 1,234,777 miles.

A classic scene at King's Cross station with three A1 Pacifics on view. No. 2795 *Call Boy* departs with the Edinburgh-bound Flying Scotsman while No. 2549 *Persimmon* on the left and No. 2579 *Dick Turpin* await their turn to depart – a shot to savour with much of interest to study. These locomotives were all named after racehorses.

Southern Railway Schools Class No. 902 *Wellington* seen in the early 1930s, before being fitted with smoke deflectors. Designed by R. Maunsell, No. 902 was one of forty of the class built between 1930 and 1935. The loco was renumbered 30902 in BR days and was withdrawn along with the other members of this class between February 1961 and December 1962.

Jubilee 4-6-0 No. 5727 *Inflexible* at St Rollox shed in 1937. A large class of 191 locos, built to William Stanier's design, they were found over most of the LMS system. No. 5727 was constructed in 1936 at Crewe and in my spotting days was an extremely scarce engine, being Scottish Region-based from 1937 until withdrawal in December 1962. (R. J. B.)

An old photograph of LNWR Precursor 4-4-0 No. 1301 *Candidate*. This class of 130 locos designed by James Whale were rated 2P or 3P if rebuilt with superheaters. All lasted long enough to carry LMS numbers and some lasted beyond 1934 and carried the later LMS numbers. The photograph pre-dates the Bakerloo line extension to Watford.

Taff Vale 'H' Class 0-6-0T No. 793, seen after its absorption into the GWR. Only three of this class were built in 1884 for use on Pwllyrehebog Incline, and they lasted until 1951, when the incline was abandoned. No. 793 is seen at Treherbert shed in 1936. (R. J. B.)

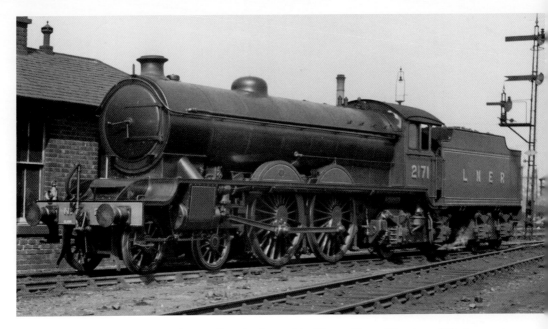

North Eastern Railway Class Z 4-4-2 No. 2171, designed by Vincent Raven. The class of fifty locomotives was designated C7 in the LNER numbering scheme and all had disappeared by 1948 without gaining British Railways numbers. This was quite an elegant locomotive to my eyes.

Adams 02 0-4-4T No. 23 at Newport shed, Isle of Wight, in 1938. Twenty-three 02s were transferred to the island between 1923 and 1949, and as a result outlasted their classmates on the mainland. All the remaining locos were withdrawn in December 1966 when the system was electrified. No. 23 carried the name *Totland*. (R. J. B.)

Beyer-Garratt 2-6-6-2T No. 7983. These articulated locos were ordered from Beyer-Peacock Ltd by the LMSR to alleviate the double-heading of freight trains on the Midland section. The thirty-three engines of the class lasted around thirty years, with the last example going in 1958.

0-4-2T Armstrong '517' Class No. 848 at Oswestry shed in 1938. 156 of these tank were built between 1868 and 1885, not all of which were similar in weight and power, but all were classified as '517'. Withdrawals were spread over many years, from 1904 until 1945. (R. J. B.)

Prototype LNER 02 2-8-0 No. 3461 is seen at the New England shed, in Peterborough. The 02 was Gresley's development of Robinson's GCR 04 Class. No. 3461 has inclined cylinders and an enlarged dome and became BR No. 63921 before being withdrawn in 1948. The other sixty-six members of the class all lasted until the 1960s.

Two fowler Royal Scot 4-6-0s are depicted when fairly new in 1937. Nos 6139 *Ajax* and 6134 *Atlas* are carrying their original names, though these would be replaced in later years by regimental ones. All seventy of the Royal Scots were rebuilt with Stanier taper boilers.

Another class of locos that saw service in the Isle of Wight were Stroudley's A1/A1X Class 0-6-0Ts. Here we see No. 8 *Freshwater* in Newport shed yard in August 1938. (R. J. B.)

The Saint Class 4-6-0s were built from 1902 and 1913. Seventy-seven engines were variously named after ladies, saints, courts and people both real and fictional. No. 2954 was named *Tockenham Court*, a manor house situated about 9 miles south-west of Swindon.

Star Class No. 4051 *Princess Helena*, seen at Swindon roundhouse, was one of a class of seventy-three engines named after such subjects as stars, knights, kings, monarchs, queens, princesses, princes and abbeys. Several of the monarch names, such as *The Japanese Emperor*, were removed during the Second World War for obvious reasons.

R. J. Billinton designed a small class of thirty locomotives for the London, Brighton & South Coast Railway, which were designated as E5. In Southern Railway days, No. 2583 is shown at Stewarts Lane (Battersea) shed in March 1939. (R. J. B.)

Great Eastern Railway 2-4-2T No. 8301. Twelve of the class were built at Stratford between 1909 and 1910, and while they were initially classified as GER Class Y65s, they later became LNER Class F7s. No. 8301 is seen at St Boswells, very far from its natural haunts, in August 1939.

V2 2-6-2 No. 4791 is seen at Ganwick, on the southern end of the LNER main line from King's Cross, while working an express in 1938. The class comprised 184 engines and was one of Nigel Gresley's most successful designs, being capable of handling express and freight trains equally.

Johnson 3F No. 3260 at Kentish Town shed. This was one of a massive class of similar locomotives that was to exceed 1,700 examples. No. 3260 was originally on the Somerset & Dorset Joint Railway line and was numbered 76 in their stock.

The LNWR E Class 2-8-0 was a rather ungainly-looking engine. Here is No. 1017, which was built as an 0-8-0 and was converted to an E in 1906. It was allocated LMS number 9605 but never carried it, being withdrawn in 1927.

An H. A. Ivatt-designed D1 Class 4-4-0, which became D2 under the LNER. Dating from 1898, the class as a whole had fairly long lives, not disappearing until 1951. Here is No. 3042 in what appears to be a posed shot, with children peering out at the photographer. Unfortunately, the location remains unknown.

4-6-0 No. 2330 *Cudworth* was a member of the N15X Class. Built as a 4-6-4 tank, the seven members of the class were all rebuilt as 4-6-0 tender engines. They were all withdrawn from service between 1955 and 1957 from Basingstoke shed. This photograph was taken at Nine Elms in March 1939. (R. J. B.)

Ex-Cambrian Railway 0-6-0 No. 878, seen at Oswestry in June 1938. Ten of these locos were built between 1894 and 1899 and all were absorbed by the GWR at the grouping in 1922. Withdrawal commenced in 1926, with the last one clinging on until 1948.

An unnamed Claughton 4-6-0 on an Up express races ahead of Prince of Wales 4-6-0 No. 25648 *Queen of the Belgians* on an Up relief near Whitmore, to the south of Crewe. No. 25648 lasted long enough to be given a BR number at nationalisation in 1948, but was scrapped shortly after, in October 1948.

Manson D42 4-4-0 No. 6872 was built by Kitson & Co. of Leeds in June 1888. Re-boiled with a Robinson superheater, she clocked up over fifty years of service before being withdrawn in December 1938. She was photographed at Kittybrewster shed in July 1933.

Maunsell Schools Class V No. 914 *Eastbourne*. Forty of these successful locomotives were built between 1930 and 1935 for work on the South Eastern section of the SR. They were displaced from there by electrification in 1959 and transferred to the South Western lines, where they lingered on for a few years, but all had gone by the end of 1962. No. 914 is decorated for the Eastbourne Jubilee celebrations of June 1933.

Douglas Earle Marsh designed these 4-4-2s for work on the LB&SCR, with twenty-seven being constructed between 1907 and 1913. The example seen here at New Cross Gate shed in September 1937 is No. 2075. This engine lasted into the BR era, becoming No. 32075, and was retired in October 1951.

200 of these chunky 0-6-2Ts were built from 1924. Designed by C. B. Collett, the locos were numbered 5600–5699 and 6600–6699. No. 6695 is seen at Solihull on a train of private coal wagons. The overwhelming majority of the class saw service in South Wales. (R. J. B.)

Royal Scot No. 6104 *Scottish Borderer* hurries through Tring on a southbound express sometime in 1929, when the loco was allocated to Camden shed. From 1931 No. 6104 moved permanently to the Scottish Region before being withdrawn in 1962; as such, it became a very rare sight south of Crewe.

Fowler LMS 2-6-2T No. 10 is pictured at Birmingham New Street in 1936. No. 10 emerged from Derby works in 1930 and on the formation of BR in 1948 it became No. 40010. It was withdrawn from Willesden shed in 1961.

The Silver Jubilee express, captured on Langley water troughs with A4 No. 2509 *Silver Link* in charge. No. 2509 was one of four locos liveried in silver and grey especially to haul this luxury train from 1935. It ran from King's Cross to Newcastle until September 1939, when the war put paid to it permanently.

Gresley LNER K3 2-6-0 No. 3832 at St Boswells in 1939. The class ran to 193 examples, which were withdrawn over a long period, starting in 1950 and ending in 1962. No. 3832 become BR No. 61992 on nationalisation in 1948. (R. J. B.)

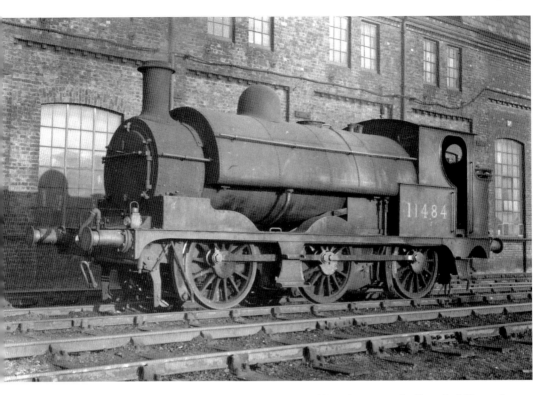

No. 11484, a Barton Wright rebuild of Aspinall's L&YR 0-6-0 saddletank, is pictured at Bury shed. Five such locos became departmental engines at Horwich works and consequently lasted much longer than other class members. No. 11305 was the last survivor, going in 1964 after eighty-seven years of service. (R. J. B.)

Southern Railway U Class 2-6-0 No. 1800 at Reading (SR) shed in June 1939. Introduced from 1928, the class consisted of seventy-one engines, of which the first twenty were rebuilds of Maunsell SE&CR Class K River 2-6-4 tanks. No. 1800 was one of those rebuilds. (R. J. B.)

No. 28, an 0-6-0 pannier tank of the Cleobury Mortimer & Ditton Priors Railway, stands at Ditton Priors station in September 1938. One of a pair of locomotives absorbed by the GWR, No. 28 carried the name *Cleobury* and No. 29 was named *Burwarton*. (R. J. B.)

0-6-0 No. 1006, as rebuilt by the GWR. Originally constructed by Beyer-Peacock in 1899 for the Midland & South Western Junction Railway as their No. 22, the loco was rebuilt in January 1926 and lasted until late 1934. These locos were the forerunners of Collett's later 2251 Class.

Raven LNER Class C7 4-4-2 No. 732, originally classified as a North Eastern Railway Class Z. Fifty locomotives in the class were built from 1911 onwards. Two were equipped with a booster in 1931 to increase tractive effort when starting, and all were withdrawn by 1948.

Although possibly outside the scope of this book, I just couldn't resist this 1891 shot of several Midland Railway '890' Class 2-4-0s at Derby No. 4 roundhouse. Only Nos 891, 69 and 107 are identifiable. This is certainly one to savour.

Webb L&NWR Cauliflower 2F 0-6-0 No. 8515 at Workington shed. These were so named because the L&NWR crest on the splasher was said to resemble a cauliflower! A long-lived class, of the 310 locos built many exceeded seventy years of service. No. 8515 lasted until February 1952 as BR No. 58398. (R. J. B.)

Worsdell North Eastern Railway Class V 4-4-2 No. 295 heads a train at Darlington in 1933. These Atlantic types became LNER Class C6. Numbering twenty, they became extinct in 1948, the last two being withdrawn in March without carrying their allotted BR numbers.

Southern D1 4-4-0 No. 1743 stands at Ashford shed in 1937. The D1 was a rebuild by Maunsell of Wainwright's SE&CR D Class. A total of seventy-two were rebuilt from 1901, of which twenty-one were rebuilt to D1. The last member of this famous class was withdrawn during 1962. (R. J. B.)

GWR Bulldog 4-4-0 No. 3353 *Pershore Plum* at Shirley station in May 1939. Quite a few of this class carried names of places on the GW system. This led to confusion among passengers, so those locos were renamed. No. 3353 was one of these, and was formerly named *Plymouth*. (R. J. B.)

LMSR 2-6-4T No. 2427 on a grey day at Accrington shed in 1939. 645 of these 2-6-4Ts were constructed to the designs of Fowler initially, then Stanier and finally Fairburn. They were all two-cylinder apart from thirty-seven three-cylinder engines built for the suburban passenger traffic on the London, Tilbury & Southend system. (R. J. B.)

Gresley K2/2 No. 4702 at Tweedmouth shed. These versatile locos were designed for the Great Northern Railway, but a large number of them gravitated to Scotland, where some carried the names of lochs. No. 4702 was never named and became No. 61792 in the BR numbering scheme. (R. J. B.)

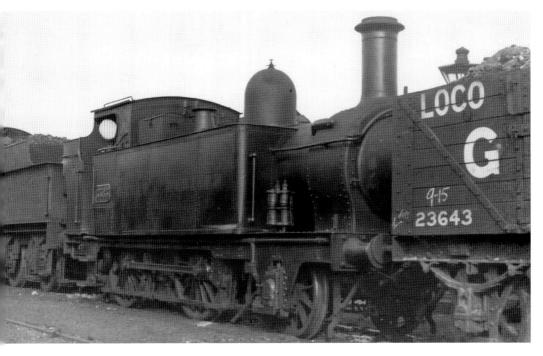

Dean 2-4-0 Metropolitan Tank No. 3583 is pictured at Oxford shed in October 1936. Constructed from 1869 until 1899, with the unusual situation of new locos still being built while earlier ones were being scrapped, ten of the class survived to see BR days. (R. J. B.)

D11/2 4-4-0 No. 6380 *Evan Dhu* is seen here at Glasgow Eastfield in 1936. The D11/2 were the post-Grouping development of Robinson's Great Central D11 Class. The D11/2s were all allocated to Scotland after a short spell on the GC section of the LNER and they carried painted names of characters from Sir Walter Scott's novels. (R. J. B.)

Stanier Princess Class No. 6200 *The Princess Royal* is seen at Oxenholme. These powerful locomotives were the first 4-6-2s to run on the LMS system and eventually totalled twelve plus the turbine-powered No. 6202, which was rebuilt as a conventional engine in 1952 only to be destroyed in the devastating collision at Harrow & Wealdstone in October 1952.

E6 Class 0-6-2T No. 2417 is seen at New Cross Gate shed in 1937. The E6 was a design by R. J. Billinton for the London, Brighton & South Coast Railway and dated from 1904. It was a smaller-wheeled version of the older E5 Class. No. 2417 became No. 32417 under BR and had a service life of fifty-seven years, being scrapped in 1963.

GWR 7200 Class 2-8-2T No. 7201. These heavy tanks weighed in at 92 tons and were C. B. Collett's rebuild of G. J. Churchward's 4200 Class 2-8-0Ts, but fitted with a larger bunker and trailing bogie wheels. No. 7201 was built in August 1930 and was withdrawn in April 1965.

Midland Railway 3P 4-4-0 No. 736 is pictured at Leeds Wellington (later Leeds City) station. A Johnson design of 1900, the class comprised eighty engines. Twenty-two locomotives survived to enter BR service in 1948, although only eight carried their BR numbers.

No. 1856 was an LNER Class J39, a class that totalled 289 engines. A Gresley design of 1926 and intended as a mixed traffic loco, they were found all over the LNER system, and were noted as being a free-running and useful class. No. 1856 finished up as BR No. 64910 and went for scrap in May 1963.

LNER Class A5 4-6-2T No. 1750, a member of the class designed by Robinson for the Great Central Railway and intended for suburban passenger work at the London end of that system. No. 1750 was one of the later Gresley-modified type that were allocated to the North Eastern area. No. 1750 later became BR No. 69833 and is seen at Darlington shed. (R. J. B.)

GWR Star Class No. 4016 *Knight of the Golden Fleece* is seen sometime in the 1920s before its rebuilding as a Castle Class locomotive. The massive nameplate is very noticeable and was later replaced by another lengthy one, *The Somerset Light Infantry*.

Dukedog 4-4-0 No. 3223 at Swindon works. Introduced as new engines, the locos of this class were in fact reconstructions using old locomotive parts, these being Duke boilers and frames from Bulldog 4-4-0s. No. 3223 was renumbered in 1946 as No. 9023 and was withdrawn in July 1957.

Royal Scot Class No. 6121 *H.L.I.* enters Northampton Castle station with a southbound train in 1934. The large No. 2 signal box is behind the train. No. 6121 gained the full version of its name in 1949, *Highland Light Infantry (City of Glasgow Regiment)*.

Wainwrights South Eastern & Chatham Class P 0-6-0T numbered just eight locomotives weighing a mere 28 tons. Intended for push-and-pull branch line working they were underpowered and ended up on shunting and station pilot duties. Four have been preserved, but not No. A558, which is seen here at Folkestone shed on October 1937. (R. J. B.)

Collett King Class No. 6000 *King George V*, fitted with a bell to mark its 1927 visit to the USA. There were thirty Kings in number and they were the principal express engines of the GWR and Western Region of BR for nearly thirty-five years until 1962, when the whole class disappeared from service.

Nos 180 and 181 were purchased for the Rhondda & Swansea Bay Railway from the Port Talbot Railway, and are seen here in GWR days. Numbered 23 and 24 by the Rhondda, they both disappeared within a brief period during 1928–29 after the Rhondda had been absorbed by the GWR.

Midland Railway 0-4-4T No. 1385 was one of 205 Johnson 1Ps, which were built from 1875. Many were equipped with the more modern Belpaire fireboxes during LMS days. Withdrawal of the class was a drawn-out affair, taking from 1919 to 1960, but No. 1385 only survived until 1948.

0-8-0 No. 9037, working a southbound coal train, is being rapidly overtaken by Jubilee No. 5594 *Bhopal,* which is on a special or relief passenger near Ashton in August 1937. Later a long-time Midland division locomotive, No. 5594 was allocated to Camden shed at this time.

D1 Class 4-4-0 No. 3062 is seen at Doncaster sometime in 1933. These engines were enlarged versions of the D2 and only fifteen were constructed. Intended for medium-load passenger work, they soon ended up on secondary duties.

Gresley Great Northern Railway J50 0-6-0 tank No. 3213. Originally GNR Class J23 they were classified J51 by the LNER until converted to J50 from 1929 onwards. The class of 102 engines remained intact until 1956, but all had gone by 1963. No. 3213 is seen at Leicester GC shed in 1939. (R. J. B.)

GWR 4-4-0 No. 3822 *County of Brecon* is pictured at Shrewsbury. Forty of these neat-looking locos were built between 1904 and 1912, and they were named after English and Irish counties. They unfortunately had fairly short lives, all going between 1930 and 1933.

Ivatt Atlantic No. 4411 was one of the famous 4-4-2s that handled much of the principal traffic on the GNR and later LNER until more powerful engines arrived. No. 4411 is seen in charge of the Harrogate Pullman near Ganwick.

Probably the best known and best design of William Stanier was the Princess Coronation Class 4-6-2s. They were the principal express power from 1937 until 1960, when diesels began to replace them. Streamlined No. 6225 *Duchess of Gloucester* is seen on Whitmore water troughs in 1939. Three of the thirty-eight locos can still be seen in preservation.

No. 193 was a Barry Railway Class K 0-6-2T, a product of the Cooke Loco Co. of New Jersey, USA. Built in 1899 along with four classmates, the locos were absorbed into the GWR. No. 193 was withdrawn during 1929.

C15 4-4-2T No. 9053 is seen at Dunfermline shed. A North British Railway design by Reid for working passenger trains, the class consisted of thirty locos built between 1911 and 1913. All had reasonably long lives, with the class not becoming extinct until April 1960. (R. J. B.)

Maunsell N Class locos were mixed traffic 2-6-0s for the South Eastern & Chatham line. Eighty locos were built from 1917 all with right-hand drive, apart from the final eight, which had left-hand drive – including No. 1407, which is seen here at Exmouth Junction shed in 1938. (R. J. B.)

William Stanier produced an 'improved' version of Fowler's 2-6-2T. 139 of these locos were produced but they showed no noticeable improvement over their predecessors in service. Pictured here is No. 176 at Holbeck shed, Leeds, in 1939.

These rather ungainly 4-6-0s were designed by C. Cumming for the Highland Railway. They were unusual for the pre-Grouping era for being fitted with the Walschaerts valve gear. Here is No. 17952 in LMS days at Inverness Lochgorm in 1938. (R. J. B.)

Saint Class 4-6-0 No. 2907 *Lady Disdain* was one of the early members of this class, which was designed by G. J. Churchward for the GWR. Built in May 1906, she was one of the earlier withdrawals as well, being withdrawn in July 1933 after having run 1,201,880 miles.

LNER D9 No. 5111 at Neepsend. Forty of these 4-4-0s were built principally to work the expresses on the London extension of the great Central line, but they were quickly replaced by Atlantic 4-4-2s. Twenty-six survived into the British Railways era.

P2 2-8-2 No. 2002 *Earl Marischal* at Aberdeen Ferryhill in May 1936. Six locos were built for work on the Edinburgh–Aberdeen section but the eight-coupled wheelbase proved too long for the curves on that line. They were soon rebuilt as 4-6-2s and in that form lasted until 1959–61. (R. J. B.)

Great Central Railway 0-6-0 saddle tank No. 154 was built at Gorton in May 1871, before being rebuilt in March 1904 and renumbered No. 154 B. The loco just made it to Grouping as an LNER Class J58, being withdrawn in October 1923.

Star Class No. 4049 *Princess Maud* at Worcester shed. Built in May 1914 and initially allocated to Old Oak Common shed, she lasted until July 1953, being withdrawn from Wolverhampton Stafford Road shed after having run 1,683,157 miles. (R. J. B.)

Stanier's heavy freight locos for the LMSR were the highly successful 8F 2-8-0s. Basically a modernised version of the GWR 2800 Class, they were found all over the LMS system and further afield. No. 8033 is seen when quite new in 1936.

Royal Scot No. 6161 *Kings Own*, sporting a hideous experiment in smoke deflection. Due to smoke drifting around the cab and obscuring the crew's view of signals, various experimental smoke deflectors were tried. This horrific version thankfully proved ineffective.

A Kitson-built 0-6-2 tank for the Rhondda & Swansea Bay Railway, No. 168 is seen at Swindon works in 1931. This was the first of nine engines and was No. 8 in the Rhondda listing. All passed to the GWR and were scrapped between 1926 and 1936.

No. 2400 was one Raven's A2 Pacifics for the North Eastern Railway, and was introduced just before the Grouping of 1923. Five of these large engines were built and each was named after a city on the North Eastern system. They were not particularly successful and had short lives, all being withdrawn by 1937.

An 0-4-0 crane tank, No. 1302, is pictured at Stewarts Lane shed. Information on this engine has proved to be very sparse, but I have found that it was one of a pair designed by J. Stirling in 1881 for the South Eastern Railway. (R. J. B.)

No. 2441 was a member of Dean's numerous GWR 0-6-0 single-frame engines known as 'Dean Goods', although they were in fact intended for mixed traffic work. Many were sent overseas during the two world wars, never to be seen again. The oldest one was No. 2340, which was withdrawn in 1954 when seventy years old.

No. 601, as an LMS 2P 4-4-0, was one of the Fowler-designed successors to Johnson's earlier 2Ps, but the locos had slightly smaller driving wheels. Few of the Johnson engines survived until the 1960s, but the LMS engines did in large number; even so, both designs became extinct in 1962. No. 601 is seen at Nottingham Midland.

Pickersgill designed his D40 4-4-0s for the Great North of Scotland Railway. Twenty-one locos of this class were built, which include the famous preserved *Gordon Highlander*. No. 6846 *Benachie*, seen at Kittybrewster in 1938, became BR No. 62274. (R. J. B.)

One of Dean's large-wheel GWR Atbara Class 4-4-0s, No. 4141 *Aden*, is seen at Salisbury in 1929. Thirty engines made up the class, which dated from 1900. They had 6-foot 8-inch driving wheels and in common with other large-wheel GWR 4-4-0s had quite short lives, varying between eleven and thirty years.

H Class 0-4-4 tank No. 1264 is seen at Stewarts Lane shed in 1939. This was a useful Wainwright design for the South Eastern & Chatham Railway, dating from 1904. Many examples were fitted for push-pull working. (R. J. B.)

Claughton 4-6-0 No. 5909 *Charles N. Lawrence* makes its smoky way south, having not long departed from Crewe. These Bowen–Cooke locos were the mainstay of the heavier trains on the LNWR and LMS until more powerful engines appeared. Only No. 6004 entered the BR era in 1948, and just for a brief time, having outlived its classmates by just eight years.

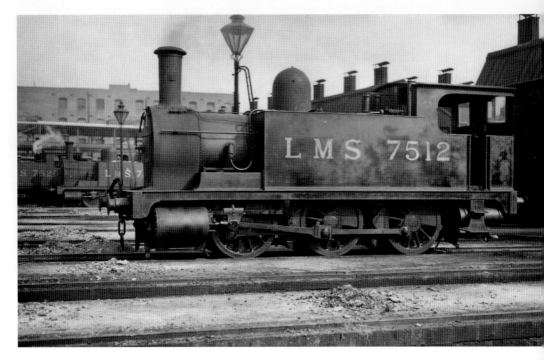

Former North London Railway 0-6-0T No. 7512 is seen at Devons Road shed. These locos were designed by J. C. Park and dated to 1887. One engine has entered preservation – No. 58850, which is based at the Bluebell Railway.

Worsdell-designed J72 0-6-0 No. 2190 is photographed at Sunderland shed in 1939. This loco was a member of a long-lived class that were in use from 1898 until 1964 with BR, with a few even lasting until 1967 as service stock. No. 2190 became BR No. 68707 and was withdrawn in April 1962. (R. J. B.)

04 Class 2-8-0 No. 6262 is seen on Charwelton water troughs on the GCR line. They were a Robinson Great Central design and over the years much modification and rebuilding led to several subclasses. No. 6262 eventually became BR No. 63819, classified as an 04/8, having been fitted with a B1 type boiler.

GWR Hall No. 5934 *Kneller Hall* at the slightly unusual location of Bournemouth shed. The Hall Class eventually numbered 330 locos, including the modified ones, although No. 4911 *Bowden Hall* was destroyed by a bomb in 1941. No. 5934 survived until May 1964.

Stanier 2-6-4T No. 2513 was a member of a class of thirty-seven engines built specifically to operate on the LT&SR section of the LMS. In this picture, No. 2513 is well off route at Northampton Castle in September 1934, possibly while still a new engine.

K3 2-6-0 No. 1158, seen fitted with indicating shelters for test purposes. Introduced in 1920, the class was Gresley's first design to be fitted with his three-cylinder conjugated valve gear. Later, they were also fitted to the highly successful A3 and A4 Pacifics. No. 1158 became No. 61915 in the British Railways numbering scheme.

One-month-old GWR 4-6-0 No. 6877 *Llanfair Grange* at Worcester shed in May 1939. The Grange Class was very similar to the Hall 4-6-0s except for having smaller driving wheels. A Grange could always be identified from a distance by the raised section of running plate over the cylinders. (R. J. B.)

No. 8813 is seen with plenty of steam to spare. George Whale designed these 4F 4-6-0s for the LNWR, with the class running to 170 engines. They dated from 1906 and were known as Whale '19-inch goods'. Only three survived to BR days in 1948, with No. 8824 being the last to go in February 1950.

A Wainwright E Class 4-4-0 is seen at Ashford shed in October 1937. The E was primarily a passenger class and was a version of the similar D Class. Eleven of the thirty-six engines were later rebuilt to E1 classification, featuring a large boiler and long travel piston valves. The last example, No. 31166, soldiered on until May 1955. (R. J. B.)

Immaculate Great Northern D3 4-4-0 No. 3400. An H. A. Ivatt design of 1896, all fifty-one members of the class were rebuilt with larger boilers from 1912 to 1928. Nineteen survived into the BR era, with three carrying their BR-allotted numbers. No. 62000 was the last to operate in traffic, going in September 1951.

GWR No. 103 was one of three French-built De Glehn compounds. No. 102 was slightly less powerful than Nos 103 and 104, and all were rebuilt with Swindon taper boilers. No. 103, named *President*, is seen in rebuilt form.

Seen at Newport Pill shed in April 1938 is former Alexandra Docks & Railway Co. No. 190. The loco and two other saddle tanks of the same type were built by Andrew Barclay Co. The total stock of the AD&R was thirty-six engines, and all were absorbed by the GWR at Grouping. (R. J. B.)

No. 17827 was one of Peter Drummond's 4F '51' Class, which were built for the Glasgow & South Western Railway. The first withdrawal of this small class occurred in 1935 and the last in was withdrawn 1947. Thus, none of the class survived into the BR era. No. 17827 is seen at Carstairs shed in May 1936. (R. J. B.)

LNER B17 4-6-0 No. 2822 *Alnwick Castle* heads the Flushing Continental boat train. This train ran from London Liverpool Street to Harwich Parkeston Quay from 1926 until the outbreak of war in September 1939. It was revived after the war and retitled the 'Day Continental'.

Southern Railway 01 No. 1093 is seen at Bricklayers Arms shed. Formerly known as the South Eastern 0 Class, many were rebuilt as 01, incorporating domed boilers and new cabs. No. 1093 was one of the rebuilds and entered BR stock, surviving until May 1951 without having its allocated BR number, 31093, applied. (R. J. B.)

Fowler 4P 2-6-4T No. 2346. Well over 100 of these rugged tank engines were produced. The later locos from No. 2395 having side-window cabs. One was named *The Prince* for a brief period in the 1930s.

Bowen-Cooke George the Fifth Class 4-4-0 No. 25409 *Dovedale*. These engines were a modified version of the earlier precursors. Three survived to Nationalisation in 1948 but they never had their allotted numbers of 58010–12 applied.

Double-framed GWR Duke of Cornwall Class 4-4-0 No. 3290 *Severn*. Sixty locomotives of this class were built, with twenty subsequently being rebuilt as Bulldog Class 4-4-0s. Others were used with parts of Bulldog locomotives to construct the 3200 Earl Class in 1936.

An LNER double-header at Guide Bridge sees Director D10 Class No. 5438 *Worsley-Taylor* piloting C1 Class No. 4420. The D10 was a Great Central design that is still represented today in preservation by the similar D11 No. 506 Class *Butler Henderson*. The C1 was one of the renowned Great Northern Atlantic 4-4-2s.

A general view of the Great Northern and later London & North Eastern locomotive shed of Hornsey around 1925, with a good array of tank and tender J Type 0-6-0s on display. Hornsey shed opened in 1899 and closed to steam in 1961.

LMS 0-8-0 No. 9568 plods through Roade station with a southbound goods train in March 1932. After the Second World War, all members of the class of 175 were allocated to the central section of the LMS, but in the 1930s they could be seen much further south, as in this photograph.

LNER Q6 0-8-0 No. 1283 at Newport (Teeside) shed in April 1939. These Raven-designed engines dated to 1913. They handled much of the heavy freight in the North East and as testament to the design some survived to the very end of steam, working in the area in late 1967. (R. J. B.)

GWR No. 359 *Hilda*, an 0-6-0 saddle tank, was built in 1917 as a one-off by Hudswell Clarke of Leeds for the Llanelli & Mynydd Mawr Railway. The name was retained until withdrawal in 1954. It was photographed at Swansea East Dock shed in September 1936. (R.J.B.)

Nearing Sharnbrook summit south of Wellingborough we see Stanier Jubilee No. 5628 *Somaliland* on a Manchester to St Pancras train in July 1936. A long-time Midland engine, No. 5628 succumbed to the scrapman in February 1963, by then having been numbered BR No. 45628.

An express leaves King's Cross in June 1933, headed by A1 4-6-2 No. 4477 *Gay Crusader*. Built at Doncaster in June 1923 as LNER No. 1477, the locomotive was rebuilt as an A3 in January 1943. Several renumberings followed and, as No. 60108, *Gay Crusader* lasted until October 1963.

A busy scene at Crewe in June 1938. Class G2A 0-8-0 No. 9312 is on what appears to be a special train – unusual work for these freight engines. Also seen is Jinty 0-6-0 tank No. 7445, which appears to be marshalling empty coaching stock.

The Southern C Class 0-6-0T was a South Eastern & Chatham Railway design of H. S. Wainwright. 109 locomotives were constructed from 1900, with the vast majority surviving into the 1950s. In this view we see a class member at Ramsgate shed in October 1937. (R. J. B.)

GWR Star Class No. 4023 *Danish Monarch* at Shrewsbury. This engine was originally named *King George*, with that name being removed when the King Class was introduced in 1927. No. 4023 was then renamed *The Danish Monarch* and finally *Danish Monarch*. The nameplate was removed in 1940 and thereafter No. 4023 ran nameless.

No. 633 was one of Fowler's 2P 4-4-0s for the LMS and Somerset & Dorset Joint Railway line. They were built between 1928 and 1932 and most lasted until the 1960s No. 633, seen at Bath shed, was one of two members of the class fitted with a Dabeg feed-water heater.

B17 4-6-0 No. 2805 *Burnham Thorpe* is seen at Parkeston shed. Seventy-three locomotives of this class were built, mostly carrying the names of stately homes or football clubs situated in LNER territory. Burnham Thorpe was the birthplace of Admiral Lord Nelson, but that didn't prevent the locomotive being renamed *The Lincolnshire Regiment*.

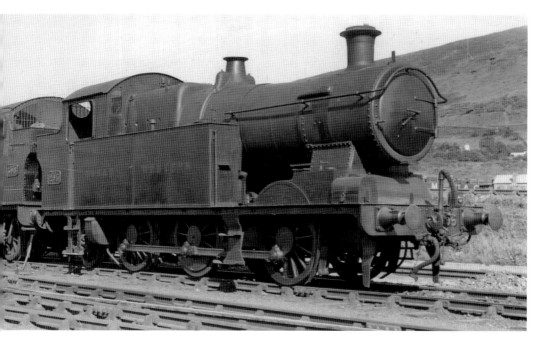

Former Taff Vale Class 04 0-6-2T No. 295 stands at Abercynon shed in July 1936. Built by outside contractors to Mr Hurry Riche's design, many were 'Westernised' after absorption by the GWR, being fitted with GWR-type boilers. No. 295 was scrapped in 1951. (R. J. B.)

A former Caledonian Railway 0-6-0T, No. 16246. Designed by J. Lambie, who died soon after, building was overseen by his successor, J. F. McIntosh. All 147 locomotives in the class – which included the slightly earlier Class 29s – survived to BR ownership. As BR No. 56246, this loco lasted until 1961. (R. J. B.)

Ivatt GNR C2 Atlantic No. 3254 pilots Robinson GCR B2 4-6-0 No. 5424 *City of Lincoln* at Doncaster in an LNER period shot from the late 1920s. The six B2s all disappeared between 1944 and 1947 and the twenty-two C2s had all gone by 1946.

GWR Castle Class 4-6-0 No. 4009 *Shooting Star*. Built as a Star Class in 1907, it was withdrawn in 1925 for conversion to Castle Class, as were fourteen other Star Class engines. No. 4009 was the first of the converted engines to be withdrawn, disappearing in 1948.

Camden bank is the location of this photo of a pair of three-cylinder compound 4-4-0s as they heave a substantial northbound express away from Euston in the late 1920s. No. 1114 is the train engine while No. 1175 lends a hand as a pilot.

The Lord Nelson 4-6-0s were a Maunsell-designed class of sixteen locomotives. All were named after famous naval commanders and when built they were the most powerful 4-6-0s in Britain. Here we see No. 856 *Lord St. Vincent* at Stewarts Lane shed. (R. J. B.)

C6 Class Atlantic 4-4-2 No. 701 at Scarborough shed in 1939. Designed by W. Worsdell for the North Eastern Railway, only two of the twenty locomotives survived to BR ownership, but not for long, succumbing in March 1948.

No. 898, a Cambrian Railway 0-6-0 built by Sharp Stewart of Manchester, is seen at Oswestry in 1939. Introduced in 1861, there were twenty-two locomotives in the class; remarkably there were forty-eight years elapsing between first and last withdrawals, the last being 1948. (R. J. B.)

LNER K2/2 2-6-0 No. 4688 works a passenger train in 1935. Sixty-five engines plus ten rebuilt from K1 comprised the class. All seventy-five entered British Railways ownership in 1948 and many lasted for years after, with the class becoming extinct during 1962.

Gresley P1 2-8-2 No. 2394 was one of a pair of large freight engines built specifically to haul heavy coal trains between Peterborough and Ferme Park, London. Massively powerful when fitted with a booster, they nevertheless had short lives, being withdrawn in 1945 after twenty years of service.

GWR Saint Class 4-6-0 No. 173 *Robins Bolitho* was the sixth built of the seventy-seven Saints and was the only member of the original engines to be named from new. It became No. 2973 and was withdrawn in July 1933 after twenty-eight years' service and 1,256,162 miles on the clock.

LMS No. 14380, a former Highland Railway Loch 2P, was a member of a class of eighteen locomotives all of which were named after Scottish lochs. Twenty years elapsed between the first and last withdrawal, which occurred in April 1950. No. 14380 was photographed at Balornock in May 1937. (R. J. B.)

No. 831, seen at Eastleigh shed in 1938, was one of the later Maunsell batch of S15 4-6-0s. Most remained in service until the mid-1960s.

No. 9757 was one of Holmes' North British Class C 0-6-0s. They were classified as J36 by the LNER and were a long-lived class, with the last few not going until 1967 – right at the end of steam in Scotland. No. 9757 is seen at an unknown location.

1901 Class 0-6-0 saddle tank No. 1963 is seen acting as station pilot at Worcester Shrub Hill in May 1939. First appearing in 1874, these numerous engines were largely rebuilt as pannier tanks. Many of them completed seventy years' service, passing to British Railways in reasonable numbers.

The first Midland compound 4-4-0s were designed by Johnson in 1901. A modified batch by Deeley followed and then a large batch of more powerful engines overseen by Fowler entered service from 1924. Here, No. 1003, one of the original engines, is seen at Kentish Town shed.

Drummond T9 Class 4-4-0s, built for the London & South Western, were elegant machines known as 'Greyhounds'. No. 733 is simmering nicely at Exeter Central in July 1938. No. 120 of this class has been preserved. (R. J. B.)

Immaculate A3 Pacific No. 2599 *Book Law* at Doncaster in September 1937. Built in 1930 and named after Lord Astor's 1927 St Leger winner, it was allocated to Haymarket or St Margarets sheds for its entire life, being withdrawn from service in October 1963 as British Railways No. 60088.

Two people can be seen watching the stately progress of GWR Saint No. 2908 *Lady of Quality*, which was photographed near Saunderton. The Saint and Star classes bore the main brunt of GWR main line expresses until more powerful motive power arrived. They then carried on in secondary service for up to thirty years.

A Jones-designed 0-6-0 for the Cambrian Railway and formerly their No. 89, now carrying its GWR number of 887 this loco is seen in showroom condition at Swindon works' B Shop in April 1932. It was withdrawn from service in November 1952.

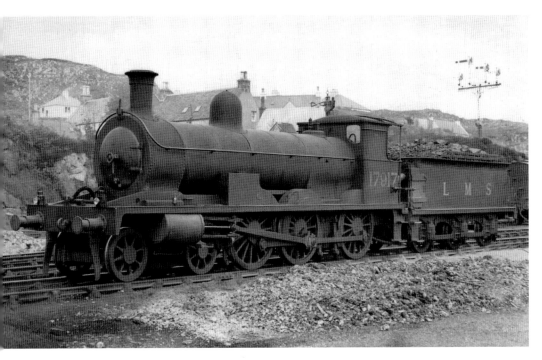

Former Highland Railway 4-6-0 No. 17917 is seen at Kyle of Lochalsh in June 1938. These locos were the first 4-6-0 wheel arrangement design to run in the British Isles when introduced in 1894. Sister loco No. 17916 still exists today, having been preserved as Highland Railway No. 103. (R. J. B.)

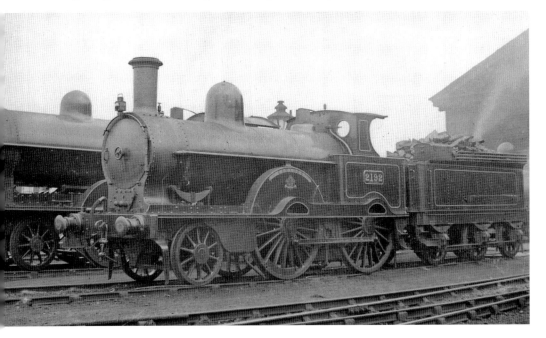

LNWR Precedent Class 2-4-0 No. 2192 *Caradoc* is here seen at Camden shed in the early 1920s. F. W. Webb designed the class, of which 166 were built from 1874. The last one disappeared in 1934, although one example, No. 790 *Hardwicke*, is preserved.

Former Great Central B6 4-6-0 No. 5052 is seen at Doncaster in 1931. Built at the company's works at Gorton in 1921, it was renumbered to LNER No. 1329, and then almost immediately to No. 1347. The loco failed to make it to BR ownership by just one month, being withdrawn in December 1947.

LNER D9 4-4-0 No. 5107 was a former Great Central Class 11B, built at Vulcan Foundry in Newton-le-Willows in 1904. Rebuilt in 1924, it later became LNER No. 2329, lasting until February 1949. It is still fitted with the GC-type chimney when seen in this photograph.

GWR No. 54 was originally a Rhymney Railway engine and became GWR property in 1922 along with the locomotives of most other small railways in the GWR area. Many of the locos were fitted with taper boilers, in what was known as 'Westernisation'. No. 54 remained in original condition, however, as seen here, at Ferndale shed in 1936. (R. J. B.)

SR X6 Class 4-4-0 No. 666 is seen at Basingstoke shed in June 1938. These rather stately looking engines, which were designed by Adams for the London & South Western Railway, numbered just ten locos, all of which were withdrawn by 1946. (R. J. B.)

No. 7757, pictured at Mold Junction shed in 1938, was an LNWR Webb 0-6-0T. Introduced in 1882, they were known as 'coal tanks', and were a very long-lived class, with many reaching sixty or seventy years of service. One of these locos is preserved.

Precursor Class 4-4-0 No. 5311 *Express* heads a diverted Up train through Northampton Castle station and takes the line to Blisworth. Gas lamps and other paraphernalia of the steam railway era abound in what is now a much-changed scene.

Gresley K2 2-6-0 No. 4661, seen at Doncaster in 1927, was one of the batch of twenty built by the North British Locomotive Company in 1918. The class were known as Ragtimers. No. 4661 became LNER No. 1751 and subsequently BR No. 61751. The end for this locomotive came in June 1959.

Two former Midland & South Western Junction locos at Swindon, post-1922. On the left is Tyrrell 4-4-0 No. 1120, but the rarity is 4-4-4T No. 25, on the right. Built by Sharp Stewart as one of a pair, this loco retained its original form, whereas the sister was rebuilt with a taper boiler. The locos were noteworthy as they were the only 4-4-4 wheel arrangement engines to ever run on the GWR.

Midland Railway 0-6-0T No. 1920 is seen at Cricklewood. This engine was one of the original sixty locos that came to be named Jintys or Humpys. Many were fitted with condensing equipment for working the London Underground Widened Lines, and No. 1920 was so fitted.

No. 492 was one of Robert Urie's G16 4-8-0T hump shunters, which wery similar in appearance to the same designer's 4-6-2T H16 Class. Both classes dated from 1921 and both lasted well in to the 1960s. No. 492 is photographed at Eastleigh shed in June 1938. (R. J. B.)

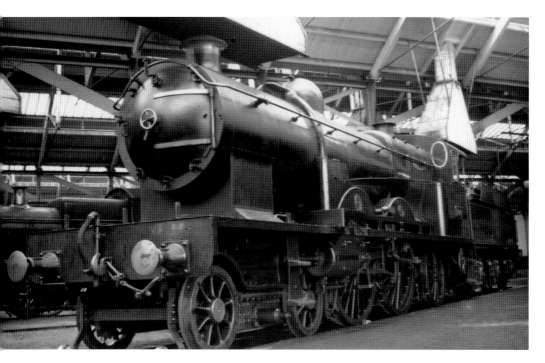

The Great Western bought three French compound 4-4-2s in the early 1900s. Built by De Glehn, they were later rebuilt with taper boilers. However, this shot shows No. 104 *Alliance* in as-built condition before 1910. All three were scrapped during the 1920s.

LNWR Experiment Class No. 165 *City of Lichfield* pilots an unidentified Claughton 4-6-0 at Huddersfield sometime before Grouping. The Experiments were Whales' last design while superintendent of the LNWR. All 105 of the engines were named after themes such as cities, counties and persons both real and fictitious.

Former North Eastern Class V 4-4-2 No. 705 (seen as an LNER Class C6) was one of twenty engines of the class built between 1903 and 1910. Only two of these elegant locomotives survived to come into BR stock in 1948, but both were soon withdrawn without having their allotted BR numbers applied.

No. 12834 stands at Lower Darwen shed. Designed by Aspinall for the Lancashire & Yorkshire Railway, these locos were classified as 6F freight engines by the LMS. A few lasted to BR days, with the loco, by then numbered BR No. 52831, being the last to survive, remaining until February 1951. (R. J. B.)

N15 4-6-0 King Arthur No. 450 *Sir Kay* at Nine Elms depot. Stronger engines than they looked, locos of this class were well able to handle the heaviest trains of the south-western section of the Southern Region. All seventy-four engines of the class carried names associated with the Knights of the Round Table. (R. J. B.)

LMS Black Five 4-6-0 No. 5158 *Glasgow Yeomanry*, seen at St Rollox shed, was one of a large class totalling 842 engines, of which only four were bestowed with names. A fifth locomotive was rumoured to have been briefly named, but no photographic evidence has been found to verify this. (R. J. B.)

Former Midland & Great Northern No. 069 stands at the Stratford works yard in March 1938. The LNER took over the M&GN locos in 1936 and the two classes of D Class 0-6-0 locos became LNER J40 and J41. Both classes became extinct in 1944. (R. J. B.)

Johnson Midland Railway 1P 2-4-0 No. 254 is seen at Saltley shed in May 1936. Out of sixty-five engines built, No. 254 was one of the eight to survive beyond 1934 and to have 20000 added to their numbers. The last example survived until 1948. (R. J. B.)

A very old photograph dating from before 1907, when this locomotive was scrapped, shows Rhymney Railway Class A No. 2. Six locos at this class (designed by T. Clements) were built by the Vulcan Foundry in 1857, and all six were scrapped in 1907 or 1908.

Experiment Class 4-6-0 No. 2638 *Byzantium* is seen at Willesden in July 1921. Built in 1909, it was renumbered 5525 in the LMS scheme. In 1934 a further renumbering to 25525 became necessary as the original number series were needed for the Patriot Class 4-6-0s, which were also being renumbered.

D30 4-4-0 No. 9499 *Wandering Willie* is recorded at Hawick shed in August 1937. The D30 was a Reid design for the North British Railway – a constituent of the LNER at Grouping. The D30s all carried names of characters associated with Walter Scott novels. (R. J. B.)

Class 02 0-4-4T No. 200 is seen parked up at Basingstoke in June 1938. These useful little tanks were around from 1899 until 1966, when the Isle of Wight Westinghouse brake-fitted examples were withdrawn. No. 200 was withdrawn in 1962 after a long seventy-one-year career. (R. J. B.)

GWR No. 1126 was a member of a small class of nine engines built for the Midland & South Western Joint line. They were absorbed by the GWR at Grouping and six of the class were rebuilt with the Swindon taper boiler, including No. 1126.

Jubilee 4-6-0 No. 5665 *Lord Rutherford of Nelson* is near Radlett on the Up Palatine from Manchester Central to St Pancras in 1939. At this date No. 5665 was allocated to Trafford Park, Manchester, but migrated to Scotland after the war, and thus became very rare for southern-based enthusiasts to see.

The locomotive rather overdoing the water pick-up is Ivatt C1 4-4-2 No. 4444, seen at Langley troughs while working a King's Cross to Cambridge train. These engines were well-regarded, although the skimpy cabs gave little protection to the crews.

A busy scene at Birmingham New Street on May 1938 with Fowler 2-6-4T No. 2351 prominent on a local working. Also seen is LMS compound No. 1164 and Patriot 4-6-0 No. 5514 *Holyhead*. All were Fowler designs or developments of older classes.

King 4-6-0 No. 6017 *King Edward IV* makes a big splash while picking up water at Rowington (Lapworth) troughs in 1929. The Kings were restricted to running over the Bicester line when working from Paddington to Birmingham and Wolverhampton.

Drummond L&SWR Class L11 4-4-0 No. 155 is seen at Eastleigh shed in June 1938. Coupled to an eight-wheel watercart tender, No. 155 would later become BR No. 30155, and although never having the number applied, would last for over three years in British Railways ownership. (R. J. B.)

Working well at Potters Bar is D2 4-4-0 No. 4397, piloting C1 4-4-2 No. 4401, which appears to be doing less work on the heavy train. Both were Ivatt Great Northern designs and had similar service lives, with the D2 Class running from 1898 to 1951 and the C1 from 1902 until 1950. The original C1, No. 251, is preserved.

LMS No. 1083 was one of Fowler's compound 4-4-0s, a modified development of the earlier Deeley design. The Fowler engines had smaller driving wheels and a higher tractive effort. A handful lasted until the 1960s but all had gone by early 1962.

Webb 2-4-2T No. 6616 is seen at Northampton Castle station on pilot or stock move duties in August 1936. At this date No. 6616 was nearly fifty years old and had another twenty years' service left to complete, being withdrawn in September 1955. It was the last of the class to remain in service.

A3 4-6-2 No. 2744 *Grand Parade* is seen somewhere on the southern end of the East Coast Main Line in the mid-1930s when allocated to King's Cross shed. Later it would migrate north of the border until being withdrawn in October 1963. Grand Parade was Lord Glanelay's 1919 Derby winner.

Claughton 4-6-0 No. 110 *Lady Godiva* at Tamworth Low Level in May 1923. Although by now an LMS locomotive, it still carries LNWR livery and number. Later numbered 6008 in the LMS scheme, it didn't survive to BR days.

Earl of Cornwall or Dukedog Class 4-4-0 No. 3205 *Earl of Devon* is seen at Swindon in 1938. Twelve of these engines were named after earls but the names were transferred to new Castle Class 4-6-0s after some of the earls complained about their names being applied to such ancient-looking engines.

Gresley A4 No. 4488 *Union of South Africa* is seen at Sandy with the Coronation streamliner five days before the declaration of the Second World War. The Coronation stated running in July 1937 between London King's Cross and Edinburgh Waverley. The train was never revived after the war.

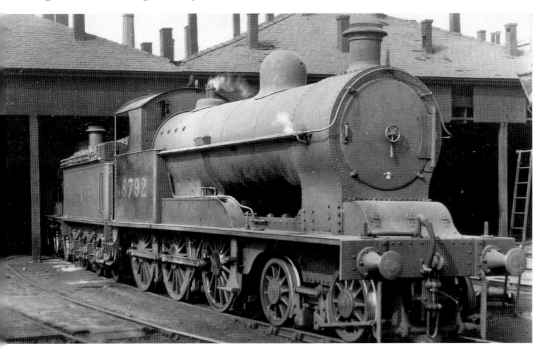

No. 8792 was one of 170 engines in Whale's LNWR 19-inch goods class, though they were really a freight version of his Experiment Class 4-6-0s. These locomotives survived to see BR service in 1948, with No. 48824 being the last to go in February 1950.

Drummond L&SWR M7 0-4-4T No. 24 is seen at Exmouth Junction in July 1938. A class of 105 engines primarily for suburban passenger and empty stock moves, they lasted in good numbers into the 1960s in the Southern Region. No. 24 became BR No. 30024 and was withdrawn in March 1963. (R. J. B.)

H2 4-4-2 No. 2426 was one of Douglas Earle Marsh's LB&SCR locomotives of 1911. This class of beautifully proportioned engines numbered just six and all were named after geological features of the south coast, No. 2426 being named *St Albans Head*. (R. J. B.)

Acknowledgments

The images in this book are from the author's collection, except for those taken by Ron Buckley, which are used by courtesy of Colin Stacey of Initial Photo Graphics, and which are captioned individually; my thanks to Colin for allowing the use of Ron's photographs. A big thanks also to Michael McGuire for typing up the manuscript, without whom this book would probably never have appeared. Also, a big thanks to the unknown photographers responsible for the other photographs; if we have inadvertently used copyright material without permission or acknowledgement, we apologise and will make the necessary correction at the first opportunity.

Sources of Information

Only original research has been used in the production of this book, which means Wikipedia 'facts' have been studiously ignored. Useful sources have been the Railways Correspondence & Travel Society Locomotive histories and particularly H. C. Casserley and S. W. Johnston's series of four *Locomotives at the Grouping* books, published by Ian Allan LTD.